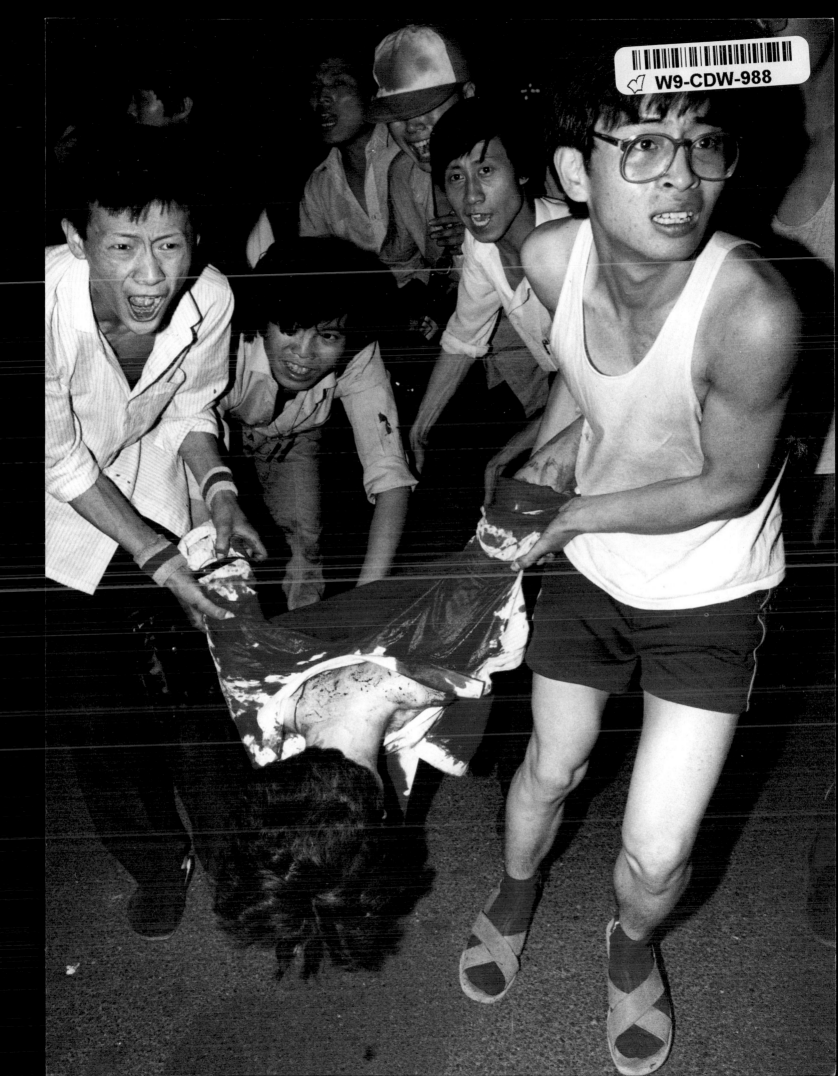

BEIJING SPRING

Photographs by
David and Peter Turnley

Text by Melinda Liu
Introduction by Orville Schell
Foreword by Howard Chapnick

Captions by Li Ming

Stewart, Tabori & Chang
New York

Published in 1989 by
Stewart, Tabori & Chang, Inc.
740 Broadway, New York, New York 10003

Library of Congress Cataloging-in-Publication
Data

Turnley, David C.
Beijing Spring.

   1. China – History – T'ien an men Incident,
1989 – Pictorial works. 2. Students – China –
Peking – Political activity – Pictorial works.
3. Peking (China) – Politics and government –
Pictorial works. I. Turnley, Peter. II. Liu,
Melinda. III. Title.
DS779.32.T87   1989   951.05'8   89-
19738

ISBN 1-55670-130-6
      1-55670-131-4 (pbk.)

Distributed in the U.S. by Workman
Publishing, 708 Broadway, New York,
New York 10003

Distributed in Canada by Canadian Manda
Group, P.O. Box 920, Station U, Toronto,
Ontario M8Z 5P9

Distributed in all other territories by Little,
Brown and Company, International Division,
34 Beacon Street, Boston, Massachusetts 02108

Produced in conjunction with ASIA 2000 Ltd.
and Black Star Publishing Company, Inc.

Printed in Japan

10 9 8 7 6 5 4 3 2 1
First edition

Page 1: Beijing, pre-dawn of June 4. <DT>

Pages 2 and 3: Demonstrators fill Tiananmen
Square. <PT>

Page 5: Daybreak in the square. <DT>

Pages 6 and 7: Early June near Tiananmen
Square. <DT>

Page 9: A mother grieves. <PT>

Frontispiece: The Goddess of Democracy
statue. <PT>

Contents

A participant in the mid-May hunger strike is carried from the square on the back of a friend. Concern for the strikers helped mobilize public support. <PT>

No one may speak for the dead; no one may interpret their dreams and visions. I have tried to fight those who would forget. Because if we forget, we are guilty, we are accomplices. . . . The world did know and remained silent. And that is why I swore never to be silent whenever and wherever human beings endure suffering and humiliation. . . . We must always take sides. Neutrality helps the oppressor, never the victim. Silence encourages the tormenting, never the tormented.

Elie Wiesel
Excerpted from his 1986 Nobel
Peace Prize acceptance speech

This is a book of remembrance. It speaks to present and unborn generations. It is a document that captures and preserves the indomitability of the human spirit and its insatiable search for freedom. It is committed to keeping memory alive, to confronting the lies of historical revisionists.

The martyrs of Tiananmen Square lie silent and still. They spoke for themselves throughout the tumultuous and chaotic weeks of the Beijing Spring of 1989. But now, in the aftermath of repression and intimidation, their symbolic Goddess of Democracy has been shattered, their banners have been removed, and their voices have been silenced.

The miracles of electronic and print journalism provided us with a dizzying progression of images that chronicled China's 1989 political morality play. We were incredulous spectators as the Chinese students dared to dream what became an impossible dream. Instant journalism captures such dramatic human events, consumes them, and spits them out to make room for the next crisis and the next disaster.

But certain events are so monumental, so symbolic, so glorious, and speak so eloquently to our highest ideals that they transcend the immediacy of the news. History demands that they be preserved. The mantle of historical responsibility resides with the journalists and photojournalists who bear witness to such events. In this book Melinda Liu describes the unfolding events in Beijing and Tiananmen Square, and Orville Schell's informed retrospection gives historical perspective to the quixotic atmosphere.

Governments understand the power of the visual image. Words may be rebutted and challenged, but photographs provide inherent evidence and defy misrepresentation. Photographers, therefore, present an immediate danger to despotic and tyrannical governments and become prime targets in the suppression of reality. It remains for the photojournalists, who produced irrefutable visual documents, to give the lie to a Chinese government that told its people and the world that no one had been shot by the soldiers in Tiananmen Square.

David Turnley and Peter Turnley are such photojournalists. Their cameras were smashed and confiscated. They and their colleagues defied open threats by the Chinese authorities to shoot on sight anyone carrying a camera. They worked twenty-four-hour days almost to the point of physical exhaustion.

Because David and Peter Turnley accept their responsibility to truth, this book was born. They see the book as a portrayal of an extraordinary event in a finite period of time. They were captivated by the energy and human dynamics that happened before their cameras. It generated in them a stamina and adrenaline-flow that helped them to work at a level of passion and dedication that they were never before able to achieve.

Were the student dissidents "hooligans," "thugs," "ruffians," and "counter-revolutionaries"? The Turnley pictures say "no." They show a peaceful, nonviolent, disciplined dissident group who never succumbed to a mob mentality. It was not an anti-Communist "bourgeois rebellion" designed to overthrow the government. It was a student protest movement, stimulated by the death of Hu Yaobang, which unleashed a drive for greater freedoms and democracy. The Turnleys photographed the coming together of a million people in one spectacular human be-in that had an inspirational, ebullient, and idealistic spirit of its own.

David and Peter Turnley's pictures undeniably attest to the bloodshed of June 3 and 4, and to the suddenly tense, angry, and dangerous mood that transformed Tiananmen Square and Changan Avenue into a battleground in a burning city. The dead bodies in the improvised morgue give their own morbid testimony to the reality.

These pictures were not made by dispassionate and uninvolved observers. Photojournalists communicate by bringing an intuitive, emotional, and visceral response to incidents that defy anticipation and logic. The unimaginable, history-making events of the Beijing Spring teach us that there is a spontaneity to the life process that circumvents photo-opportunities and media control. They point up the fraternal beauty of the photojournalistic profession and the mutual dependency of photojournalists when surrounded and threatened by hundreds of tanks and armored personnel carriers and thousands of soldiers with automatic machine guns.

The publishers, writers, and photographers of this volume believe that the assembled words and pictures are a testament to the Chinese students, living and dead, who, with innocence and naivete, shook the basic foundations of a totalitarian government.

HOWARD CHAPNICK
July 1989
New York City

A soldier of the People's Liberation Army watches the events on the streets of Beijing. <PT>

Introduction

As people around the world struggled to articulate their feelings in the aftermath of the June 4 massacre of democracy demonstrators in China, the word that was most often repeated was "tragic." The final bloody denouement of this extraordinary nonviolent protest did, indeed, have an ending that was deeply tragic, no matter what perspective it was viewed from. It was tragic for the students who were wounded and killed, tragic for the government who killed them, and tragic for the world that China had once again been thrown to the brink of chaos. But the longer-term and more fateful tragedy for China was that in a single day the country was propelled out of a hopeful era of reform, which began ten years ago just after Deng Xiaoping had ascended to power, back into just the sort of grim and chaotic revolutionary condition that had so plagued it throughout the first half of this century.

In making this sudden and precipitous transition, China crossed a line that will doubtless come to be viewed by historians as one of the seminal moments of its long and unsuccessful effort to develop and democratize. By losing the hope of reform, China also lost, at least for now, the hope of modernizing peacefully. It lost yet another generation of young Chinese intellectuals who, educated abroad and filled with energy and patriotism, might have been the country's salvation. But they have been forced underground or into exile in order to avoid arrest, imprisonment, and even execution, and once again China has deprived itself of a whole new generation of its best and brightest.

For a while, it looked as if China had succeeded in breaking out of its old historical pattern of failed reform, which had repeated itself over and over ever since the failure of the Hundred Days Reform in 1898 at the end of the Qing Dynasty. Then, under the influence of a group of progressive-minded literati, the young Guangxu emperor had attempted a blitz of modernizing reforms, only to have them terminated in a counterattack by palace conservatives who, after executing many of the key reformers and forcing others into exile, promptly tried to restore the status quo ante. There have been repeated pogroms against intellectuals and dissenters since: the bloody Shanghai White Terror in 1927, when Chiang Kai-shek turned against his Communist allies; his continued brutal suppression of those with dissenting views in the thirties and forties; the first "rectification campaign" launched by Mao's young Chinese Communist party in 1942, in which many open-minded thinkers were purged; the savage "anti-rightist" campaign in 1957, during which hundreds of thousands of intellectuals with "incorrect" views were "sent down" to the countryside in exile. All have meant that, again and again, China has been denied the abilities of just that class of educated, thoughtful people upon whom the modernization of any society inevitably depends.

But the final tragedy of such violent repression of such peaceful protests is that, until the government of Deng Xiaoping and his clique of aging comrades in arms either falls or is radically reconstituted, there is no way for anyone to express, much less redress, grievances, other than engaging in acts of violence. If they do not join the new Chinese diaspora, those young people in China who had been reanimated by the ideals of democracy and freedom of expression are left with only two alternatives. They can surrender and seek to live unobtrusive and obedient lives in order to avoid retribution from the party. Or they can go underground to organize an opposition to carry out acts of sabotage against the government, just like those early followers of the Chinese Communist party once did. In its own way, each alternative is brutalizing. To say and do nothing against a government that has been so demonstratively corrupt, inept, and repressive would be a violation of any person's humanity. But to act against it would demand an underground existence filled with fear and violence. If China's current leaders, who once lived just such lives during the struggle of the Chinese Communist movement against Chiang Kai-shek and the Nationalists, are any guide, those who are forced to live underground pursued by the police do not long keep their own humanity. Regardless what ideology they espouse, when their time comes to rule, people who have led such brutalized lives, though themselves once oppressed, all too easily turn into oppressors.

As the photographs of David and Peter Turnley show so graphically, the atmosphere in Tiananmen Square before martial law was declared was the exact opposite of what it was afterward. Imbued with a sense of hopefulness, euphoria, and affability, no one talked of violence or of overthrowing the government. There was sweetness and naivete to the students, and a moderate beseeching quality to both their demeanor and their demands. But as soon as troops started entering Beijing, things began to change. And by the time of the massacre on June 4, vengeful pessimism fully replaced the gentleness and optimism that had been so obvious just days before. Defoliated of any more dreams of peaceful and piecemeal change in China, a whole generation of Chinese suddenly found itself irreconcilably in opposition. China was plunged into the same kind of darkness that harkened back to the days when the current generation of China's leaders were, because of their own dissenting political views, living underground and hunted like wild animals by the police.

In 1930, China's most renowned contemporary essayist, short-story writer and poet Lu Xun, had himself been forced to flee and hide from the White Terror of the Nationalists. In the winter of 1931, when he heard that a group of young Chinese writers had been executed by the government in Shanghai's Longhua prison, he was filled with despair for China's future. He composed an untitled poem (written, he said, "for the sake of forgetting") that is hauntingly suggestive of the same anguish that intellectuals are once again feeling over their country's latest tragedy.

> *I am growing accustomed now to these endless nights of spring,*
> *Fleeing with my wife and child, my hair turning gray.*
> *In dreams I make out a loving mother's tears,*
> *While on the ramparts of the city the banners of the ruling warlords*
> *   are forever changing.*
> *Watching as this generation of my friends is turned into ghosts,*
> *Angrily I try and snatch a poem from all the swords.*
> *But once recited, I must bow my head, for there is no place to*
> *   write it down.*
> *Moonlight like water reflects off my black robe.*

Lu Xun's vision of China was a dark one, but one that now, sadly, has acquired a new relevance as once again a repressive and inept government drags China down toward disassembly. No longer able to hope for reform as their country's salvation, Chinese intellectuals have little to look forward to other than the fall of their government.

ORVILLE SCHELL
July 20, 1989
San Francisco

PAGES 22 AND 23:

In a show of strength that continued for several days after the crackdown on June 4, army tanks patroled Changan Avenue, often firing at anything that moved. <PT>

21

The death of Hu Yaobang was the event that first brought students to Tiananmen Square. Though forced to resign as secretary general of the Communist party in 1987, Hu had continued to lobby for political reform for the rest of his life. <PT>

Beijing Spring:
Loss of the Mandate of Heaven

For years the image of socialism hasn't been good, and not only in China. This is a fact. The rate of economic development has not been fast. And there have been some problems, politically speaking, in the field of democracy and human rights.

Those words were spoken by Hu Yaobang, then secretary general of the Chinese Communist party, near the end of a candid interview he gave in September 1986 to a group of editors from *Newsweek* and the *Washington Post*. At the time there was little hint in those simple words of the role that Hu, and China's democracy movement, would play in the cataclysmic drama to come.

Within a few months, student protests erupted in Beijing and other cities in China, and Hu lost his post for not dealing harshly enough with the unrest. Hu's statement, which appeared at the time to be unassailable fact, was thrown back in his face as evidence of his serious "mistakes" by rivals who purged him. He had failed to defend socialist ideology against the "sugar-coated bullets of the bourgeoisie," it was said. Afterwards, Hu became a liberal champion for the intelligentsia, an increasingly vocal advocate of democratic change.

In the spring of 1989, Hu Yaobang's death triggered one of the most convulsive episodes in the forty-year history of the People's Republic of China, an upheaval remarkable in scope and seismic in intensity. From April to June during that Beijing spring, the nation of 1.1 billion charted violent moodswings. Hu's funeral gave birth to a mass movement. A historic Sino-Soviet summit catalyzed a near-revolution. And a fierce power struggle ended in bloody confrontation between an army of the people and the people it was supposed to protect.

IN THE BEGINNING

In feudal times, before the last imperial dynasty toppled in 1911, Chinese believed that unusual events, such as natural disasters and peasant uprisings, foreshadowed the loss of the emperor's supernatural endowment of power. That superstition persisted long after the Communist Red Army swept to power forty years ago, when Mao Zedong announced to the world from Tiananmen Square that the Chinese people had stood up. In 1976, Chinese pointed to the earthquakes and political turmoil preceding Mao's death as proof that he, too, had lost the "mandate of heaven." Similarly, Chinese now believe the Beijing Spring of 1989 and its ruthless suppression mark the beginning of the end for the regime of Deng Xiaoping.

The tragedy of Tiananmen Square is especially ironic given Deng's own political history. Purged three times as a "capitalist roader," Deng's performance as a canny political survivor often relied on the support of the people. The masses had rejoiced when Deng clawed his way back to power a decade ago, after Mao's demise and the fall of the ultraleftist Gang of Four. Even while the feisty leader from Sichuan was still in disgrace, Beijing residents had signaled support for Deng Xiaoping by surreptitiously leaving small bottles – *xiao pingzi* in Chinese, a homonym of his name – in public places, such as in Tiananmen Square.

Deng's trademark was the policy of the open door. He introduced Western imports and sent thousands of Chinese students abroad. He welcomed foreign investment and market reforms, dividing cumbersome "people's communes" into family farms and freeing private enterprise from its Maoist stigma. He normalized relations with the United States. He even invited a cautious rapprochement with the Soviet Union, which culminated in Soviet president Mikhail Gorbachev's visit to Beijing for the first Sino-Soviet summit in thirty years.

Politically, too, Deng relaxed the rigid orthodoxy of the 1966-1976 Cultural Revolution, but only enough to justify his economic plans. "It doesn't matter if a cat is black or white as long as it catches mice," said Deng in defense of his economic pragmatism. At times Deng appeared sanguine about the negative side effects of the "open door" policy. "When you fling open the window," he went so far as to say, "some flies and mosquitoes are bound to fly in."

But Deng remained a tragic figure. Although he had resuscitated China's moribund socialist economy with an injection of market forces, he had promoted economic reform while stifling its political counterpart. Deng's economics-only approach failed to satisfy China's crisis of rising expectations. As their material standards and economic power grew, so did the Chinese people's desire for a greater say in their own future. They yearned for greater accountability and openness from a regime that had grown sclerotic, isolated, and corrupt.

China's increasing social diversity was in full evidence in the early spring of 1989. In one Beijing park, young couples twirled their way through the intricate steps of stylized ballroom dancing. Free markets bustled with buyers and sellers of imported goods. Western literature, films, and even television soap operas were common fare for urban Chinese. Spring fashion was a profusion of mini-skirts and lace stockings, faded jeans and running shoes.

But a crisis brewed behind the crimson walls of the Zhongnanhai leadership compound, northwest of Tiananmen Square. A succession scenario that Deng, now eighty-four, had painstakingly crafted over the past decade was in tatters. Deng had been compelled to sack Hu, his handpicked successor, in January 1987 for being too lenient during a wave of street demonstrations. Another heir apparent, former premier Zhao Ziyang, succeeded Hu as party secretary general but was now under attack. Deng seemed prepared to sacrifice Zhao, too.

Conservative rivals blamed Zhao, an advocate of market reforms, for a plague of economic dislocations. The most critical stage of China's economic restructuring – price reform – had hit an impasse. The regime had hoped to phase out low, subsidized prices set by the state in favor of prices determined by supply and demand. The reforms stalled halfway, however, and as a result the cost of many commodities fluctuated between the old-fashioned state-set price system and a developing black market. As a result, prices spiraled upward and inflation rampaged as high as thirty percent in some cities.

As Chinese strove to get rich quick, many bureaucrats found that corruption helped them get richer quicker. Official graft and profiteering burgeoned out of control. Authorities exploited their official access by purchasing goods at low state-set prices and re-selling them on the open market for a tidy profit. Meanwhile, the wages of urban factory workers, civil servants, and the intelligentsia stagnated in comparison with the growing wealth reaped by corrupt officials, private entrepreneurs, and rural peasants who had seen their incomes skyrocket after Deng had allowed them to farm privately once again. University students, despite their elite status, studied under grim conditions in cash-strapped universities, routinely crowded into squalid dormitories of bleak concrete and reeking communal lavatories. Their professors earned a mere U.S. $82 a month.

A DEATH ON APRIL 15

Against a backdrop of inequity and dissatisfaction, Chinese politics seemed to mimic the ancient parables in which scholar-officials sacrificed their lives to bring an errant emperor to his senses. Hu Yaobang assumed the scholar-official role, and his student supporters took up the part after his death.

After being forced to resign as party head in 1987, Hu had remained a member of the powerful Politburo and had continued to lobby for political reform. In early April 1989, during a Politburo meeting, Hu repeatedly attempted to read a long, rambling list of government misdeeds, including corruption, nepotism, and other abuses of power. But Hu's colleagues paid little heed. Economist Yao Yilin made as if to walk out of the meeting. Even moderate leader Zhao Ziyang asked Hu to get to the point. Hu lost his temper and declared, "We have failed the people and the nation." Then, as the Politburo watched aghast, Hu collapsed of a heart attack and was rushed to a hospital. He died a week later, on April 15, at the age of seventy-three.

Beijing students proclaimed Hu to be "the soul of China" and streamed into the streets to mourn him. They lay white funeral wreaths around Hu's portrait on the white obelisk in the middle of Tiananmen Square. They marched on Zhongnanhai, staging sit-ins around the leadership compound, and tolerated beatings by police wielding truncheons and electric prods when they refused to be bused away from the square. Echoing the grievances that Hu had tried to address, the activists called for democratic freedoms, a crackdown on corruption, and greater state funding for education. In particular, they demanded a freer press and resumption of now-stalled political reforms, such as the unprecedented registration of multiple candidates for local congress elections that was allowed in 1987.

Many protestors carefully acknowledged the leadership of China's Communist party, and the impracticality of trying to graft American-style democracy onto their society. Even so, the display of public dissent irked China's elderly leaders. So did subtle signs of more specific opposition. One wall poster on a university campus stated, "Those who should have died, haven't died." And protestors left Tiananmen Square littered with broken glass from small bottles that they had smashed.

DEFIANCE

Deng's response to the students was harsh. During a party meeting in late April, he lambasted the unrest as "an organized conspiracy to create turmoil." That speech was the basis for a shrill editorial published the next day, on April 26, in the party mouthpiece, *People's Daily*. It accused students of instigating "social turmoil" and of plotting to overthrow the leadership of the Communist party.

The commentary enraged protest leaders, who described their movement as "patriotic and democratic." Instead of intimidating the students, the editorial inflamed even larger protests. Demonstrators no longer simply mourned Hu; they became increasingly angry at Deng. They camped out all night in Tiananmen Square and the next day more than one hundred thousand demonstrators thronged the streets of the capital to mark the funeral of Hu Yaobang. They demanded to meet premier Li Peng after the funeral service; he avoided them.

Hu's death also exacerbated rifts within the Chinese leadership. All five members of the Politburo Standing Committee had approved the crucial April 26 editorial, including Zhao Ziyang, who received a copy during a week-long visit to North Korea. But upon returning to Beijing in early May, Zhao had a change of heart. He described the editorial as "too strident," according to party documents. And on May 3 he delivered a party speech that ignored conservative recommendations for a denunciation of "bourgeois liberalism," the Chinese catchphrase for liberal practices from the West.

Another massive demonstration erupted on May 4, the seventieth anniversary of a historic campaign by students and intellectuals in the name of democracy and science. The 1919 May Fourth Movement had protested the weak-kneed diplomacy and corruption of China's early republican government and had forced it to reject the Versailles peace treaty, which ceded most of the Chinese province of Shandong to Japan. Considered the precursor of the Chinese Communist movement, the original May Fourth campaign introduced nationalism, public opinion, and mass protest as potent forces in Chinese politics. It continued to inspire the Tiananmen demonstrators.

As tens of thousands of protestors poured into the streets of the capital on May 4, it became clear that the movement was growing in defiance of the authorities. That day, Zhao Ziyang took an irreversible step. Addressing more than two thousand governors of the Asian Development Bank in the Great Hall of the People, Zhao adopted a conciliatory stance toward the students. He described their grievances as "reasonable" and their movement as patriotic. That helped momentarily defuse the crisis; many students returned to class. But the speech ruffled Zhao's Politburo colleagues. A secret party document circulated among top officials said Zhao's remarks "represented his own views," meaning that he had strayed dangerously from the policy set by Deng.

Despite their obvious discomfort, China's leaders had ruled out a heavy-handed crackdown to avoid spoiling the upcoming visit by Mikhail Gorbachev, to begin May 15. The week before Gorbachev's visit was punctuated by a series of protests around the city. A hundred journalists converged on the state-run Xinhua News Agency to protest media censorship of the recent demonstrations. A petition signed by one thousand Chinese journalists called for more comprehensive coverage of developments in the democracy movement and talks on press freedoms. That was a common demand: under the taut rules of party censorship, China's media had remained toothless, despite considerable relaxations during Deng's rule. Editors and reporters could be fired, or their newspapers shut down, if they published articles that attacked individual leaders by name or criticized the ruling party in too pointed a manner.

In April, a courageous editor named Qin Benli dared to publish pro-democracy commentaries in the *World Economic Herald* in Shanghai. One praised Hu Yaobang and charged that his ouster was illegal. The newspaper was suspended by order of Jiang Zemin, then party boss of China's largest and most cosmopolitan city. (He later replaced Zhao as party secretary general.) During the protests of May, hundreds of journalists from prestigious publications in Beijing and Shanghai marched to demand press freedoms and Qin Benli's reinstatement. "Why should Chinese reporters act like grandchildren of the government?" demanded a Beijing journalist surnamed

Xu, who had quit his job at a Chinese magazine in protest.

Anti-corruption reforms were another insistent demand of the Beijing Spring. Protestors wanted public disclosure of the incomes of top-ranking leaders and their families, an end to nepotism, and prosecution of authorities found abusing their privilege for material gain. "Without corruption, prices wouldn't rise," proclaimed banners in the streets.

The campaign against nepotism and abuses of power tarnished both Deng and Zhao, whose sons were accused of exploiting their powerful connections in order to do business. Deng's son Pufang – who was thrown out of an upper-story window by radical Red Guards during the Cultural Revolution and was crippled as a result – headed an organization for the handicapped and was rumored to profit handsomely from it. Zhao's son was heavily criticized for allegedly pulling strings to benefit commercial dealings in southern China.

One joke that made the rounds in May had Deng discussing the mettlesome student protests with Zhao. "All we need to do is kill a few young people, and this unrest will be finished," Deng announces.

Aghast, Zhao asks, "How many? Twenty?"
Deng shakes his head.
"Two hundred?" Deng says no again.
"Two thousand?" asks the agitated Zhao.
Deng replies: "No, only two."
Relieved, Zhao responds, "Which two?"
Deng answers: "Your son and my son."

THE SUMMIT

Gorbachev's visit offered a unique tactical opening for the protest movement. On May 13, a couple hundred university students pedaled to Tiananmen Square on bicycles and launched a hunger strike around the marble obelisk known as the Monument to the People's Heroes.

The protestors demanded a sincere dialogue with government representatives, a retraction of the hard-line April 26 *People's Daily* editorial, and official recognition of their Autonomous Federation of Beijing's Universities Students. Too late, Chinese authorities realized the hunger strikers, whose motley banners and university flags now flapped insouciantly from official flagpoles around the obelisk, could trigger a diplomatic fiasco. In a last-ditch attempt to end the sit-in before Gorbachev arrived, moderate government officials affiliated with Zhao Ziyang visited student leaders in the square and asked them to return to campus. But the talks broke down.

As a result, Gorbachev touched down to an unusual sort of hero's welcome. Protestors surged through Tiananmen Square, just meters from the Great Hall of the People where some of the Soviet leader's key meetings were scheduled. Crowds lined his limousine routes. University students petitioned to meet him. (Knowing it would tarnish the summit, Gorbachev declined.) Red banners in Chinese characters and Cyrillic script hailed Gorbachev as "the true reformer."

The Soviet leader's enthusiastic reception was a backhanded slap at his Chinese hosts, whose successes in economic reform were accompanied by an acute failure to introduce, or even acknowledge a need for, political reforms of the sort that Gorbachev's "glasnost" welcomed.

What the Soviets saw in Tiananmen Square was both exhilarating and terrifying, a vision of glasnost gone amok. Both Chinese and Soviet officials tried to endure the awkwardness of the situation by studiously ignoring the Tiananmen turmoil, at least officially. When a journalist asked Raisa Gorbachev if she had seen the square, she evaded the issue with the airy statement: "There are so many squares in China." A Russian diplomat was breathless. "There are banners saying 'the Soviet Union has Gorbachev, but who does China have?'" marveled the awestruck envoy during a private moment. "It's unbelievable." The tumult was impossible to ignore. Gorbachev's schedule changed time and again because of the mass of demonstrators. His official host, Chinese president Yang Shangkun, was forced to scrabble together a hasty welcoming ceremony at the airport instead of in Tiananmen Square. At one point Gorbachev was virtually sneaked into the Great Hall of the People through a little-used back entrance.

A wreath-laying ceremony at the Heroes' Monument was canceled. So was a tour of the Forbidden City and a night of Beijing Opera. Even the parting press conference shifted suddenly from the Great Hall to the State Guest House – but only after most journalists had already arrived at the first location. The last-minute changes infuriated Yang Shangkun, who later harped on Beijing's loss of face and international prestige as one reason for the crackdown.

Beijing's turmoil quickly upstaged the summit. During Gorbachev's four-day visit, demonstrators thronged Tiananmen Square daily, despite scorching sun and sudden thunderstorms. By midweek, the mass of hunger strikers had swollen to three thousand, and a million demonstrators converged to demand free speech, clean government, and democratic rights. Every morning, more and more protestors poured out of the Beijing railway station from the provinces. Sympathetic train conductors had allowed them to ride for free.

What was intended as a foreign-policy victory for Deng became an acute embarrassment. Fortunately for the course of state relations, both sides had

On the second day of Mikhail Gorbachev's visit to Beijing, he met with Zhao Ziyang, then secretary general of the Communist party. Not long after the summit, Zhao fell out of favor for his support of the students and, on June 23, officially lost his post. <PT>

hammered out the most important diplomatic points long ago. Gorbachev's May 16 meetings with Deng Xiaoping marked the full normalization of Sino-Soviet relations after a three-decade-long chill. Cast in the role of a junior supplicant, Gorbachev politely deferred to his octogenarian host during the largely ceremonial encounters.

Walking into a banquet, Deng displayed flashes of his old charisma. He spontaneously grabbed Gorbachev and his wife Raisa each by the hand, and posed for photographs with a childlike smile. Later, however, onlookers reported that the Chinese leader's hands twitched, his mind wandered, and morsels of food occasionally eluded his chopsticks.

Gorbachev ironically found more of a soul mate in Zhao Ziyang, who struck a sympathetic chord by stating: "Political reform and economic reform should basically synchronize; it won't do to lag behind in political reform."

But Zhao had his own hidden agenda. He pointedly stressed to Gorbachev that Deng was still China's "Helmsman," a phrase normally reserved for the late Chairman Mao. Zhao even cited a secret central committee decision in 1987 – when Deng retired from key posts – to continue to defer to Deng on major decisions. It was a clear attempt to blame China's current troubles and whatever loomed ahead on Deng.

While Gorbachev and well over one thousand foreign journalists remained in town, Chinese authorities handled the raucous festival of democracy with tolerance. Traffic police with white gloves and long-haired student marshals directed traffic together along specially cordoned emergency routes, called "lifelines," for ambulances carrying ailing hunger strikers. Citizens donated quilts and tents. Doctors set up a makeshift field hospital. The Red Cross mobilized nearly one hundred city buses for protestors to use as shelters from the rain. The spirit of Tiananmen proved infectious; similar protests spread to at least thirty-four cities. The aura of innocence evoked a sort of Far Eastern Woodstock: there was a naive optimism that positive change toward democratic concepts common in the West was within reach. One student from Beijing's prestigious Qinghua University wandered around holding a poster with the English lyrics from a Joan Baez song; the T-shirt of another read "we shall overcome." "We were so peaceful, so honest," admitted student leader Wu'er Kaixi later, after the bloodletting.

The demonstrators stressed their desire to improve the existing system, not overthrow it. At the core of the protest movement was a sense that forty years of socialism had not delivered on its own promises of equitable livelihood and a government accountable to the people. Yet the demonstrators' game plan was soft on specifics. Given China's lack of a democratic tradition, the students gleaned ideas from a hodgepodge of sources, from the writings of Thoreau to the U.S. civil rights movement, from Gandhi's creed of nonviolence to images of South Korean anti-government protests shown on television. "I don't know what democracy is," declared one Beijing woman, "but China needs more of it."

WITH THE MASSES

What had begun as a relatively isolated student movement had now blossomed into the leadership's worst nightmare: an alliance between activist students and restless urban workers. Informal strikes paralyzed the capital. Slogans never before heard publicly were shared by steel workers in hard hats, computer technicians, and the national volleyball team. "Deng Xiaoping, your mind is muddled. Step down and go play bridge," admonished a flag draped across the hood of a commandeered bus packed with cheering workers. One poster stated simply, "Deng Xiaoping, thanks and good-bye."

That the demonstrators dared denounce Deng in public was a measure of China's generation gap. Many were too young to be impressed by Deng's revolutionary credentials, or his role in ending the scourge of the Gang of Four. One of them, an eighteen-year-old pedicab driver named Wang, had worked nonstop for three days transporting students for free. As he pedaled past the square one night, Wang asked abruptly, "Do you know why people are in the streets?" he asked with indignation. "It's because of the corruption of state leaders." Wang alleged that Deng and his son had salted away millions of dollars in a foreign bank account, charges widely believed by protestors, though virtually impossible to confirm. Joked another demonstrator: "It doesn't matter whether a cat is black or white as long as it resigns."

Such irreverence was ample proof that Chinese, who had been granted an increasing measure of economic power from the socialist state, now yearned for some political breathing space as well. Some of the most active protestors were private entrepreneurs. Reviled in Mao's day as "capitalist tails that must be chopped off," family enterprises such as restaurants and even modest factories had flourished under Deng. Without political commissars to reinforce the party line, they proved to be a breeding ground for protest. In Beijing, three to four hundred private entrepreneurs organized a motorcycle brigade, dubbed the "Flying Tigers," and roared around town passing messages and monitoring troops for the democracy movement.

City dwellers, who had watched their salaries stagnate in the face of rampant inflation, added their voices of dissent. With civil servants marching behind their units' flags, the Chinese bureaucracy seemed to be unraveling. Filing in columns down Beijing's wide avenues were employees of the national airlines, the China Travel Service, the Foreign Ministry, even the cadre school of the Communist party. "Don't be a vault for corruption," admonished a white vertical banner draped on the side of the official Bank of China.

Such public displays of support exhilarated the students, whose previous protests in 1986 and 1987 had not succeeded in galvanizing the masses. "Our past movements failed, but now we have more confidence and maturity," said a white-frocked medical student. "We have an autocracy now. What we want is democracy, and the people support us."

The protestors even boasted a nascent bureaucracy. Specialized groups were assigned to the broadcasting station, the sanitation committee, the media group. Students from out-of-town colleges poured out of the train stations and marched to the nearby square behind fluttering school flags. There, monitors formed vast concentric security rings, organized school by school, to protect the hunger strikers. They required visitors to pass through "security checks" that, in the inner sanctum near the broadcasting system, involved passes embellished with the official seal of the student leaders.

Inside one of the cordons, Beijing Normal University student representative Wu'er Kaixi, twenty-one, slumped across a mound of clothes, too weakened by hunger to give an interview. Normally brash and charismatic, Wu'er Kaixi was perhaps the best known – and after the crackdown the most wanted – of Beijing's student leaders. But he hardly seemed a dangerous rebel. His father was a loyal member of the Communist party and Wu'er Kaixi himself once indicated he hoped to join the party too. A member of the Uighur minority group, he read classical Chinese novels and had a poetic bent. But his cocky irreverence branded Wu'er Kaixi a troublemaker in the eyes of government officials. Later, after the massacre, state television aired video footage of him dining with visitors in a hotel restaurant to imply he had feasted during the hunger strike; in fact, the scene had been filmed surreptitiously after the fast had ended.

As public order deteriorated, the Chinese power struggle headed for a climax virtually as soon as Gorbachev's Beijing schedule ended on May 18. (The Soviet leader flew to Shanghai that day en route to Moscow.) In an emergency meeting of the country's top leaders before dawn, Zhao continued to push for concessions for the students, including an immediate dialogue and an anti-corruption campaign that would begin with his own family. Deng and other conservatives refused. At one point Deng warned his protégé ominously, "I have three million troops behind me." Zhao countered bravely, "I have all the people of China behind me." Deng's chilling riposte: "You have nothing."

Still hoping to avoid catastrophe, Zhao and other Chinese officials visited convalescing hunger strikers in two Beijing hospitals that morning. The leaders ministered to the ailing students, wiping brows and patting wrists. But the hunger strikers grabbed the opportunity for debate. "It's your duty to fight corruption," retorted one reclining patient, "You should start with your own sons." Another student rebuked Politburo member Hu Qili, "We asked to meet you three times." Hu replied, "We were busy that day with Mr. Gorbachev."

In another concession that afternoon, Premier Li Peng met with disheveled student representatives in the Great Hall of the People for an hour-long, televised dialogue. For the students, it was a measure of their growing public support and impressive ability to maintain order and a sense of purpose in Tiananmen Square, which was now literally jammed with demonstrators.

But both sides mishandled the opportunity, and their differences could not have been more glaring. Dressed in a stern Mao suit, Li raised his voice aggressively and lectured the students about impending chaos. "In Wuhan, students have already stopped the trains for three hours," warned Li. "We've experienced turmoil many times in China: people don't intend it but it happens. We will not sit idly by, doing nothing."

The students – sporting jeans and headbands, long hair and leather jackets – remained defiant. Dressed in pajamas and clutching an oxygen bag, Wu'er Kaixi interrupted Li Peng brusquely, "We don't have much time to listen to you. Thousands of hunger strikers are waiting. Let's get down to the main point. It is we who invited you to talk, not you who invited us – and you were late." Wu'er Kaixi said the student leadership was eager to leave the square, but first the April 26 editorial had to be retracted and the protest movement acknowledged to be patriotic. Li Peng, clearly irked, failed to offer further concessions and ended the meeting with a terse "good-bye."

At 4:50 A.M. on May 19, Zhao made a dejected farewell visit to Tiananmen Square. In yet another pre-dawn emergency session of Chinese leaders, he earlier had been effectively ousted from power by Deng and his colleagues in the Politburo. Zhao insisted on a final meeting with the students, and sped off despite opposition from Politburo members. Li Peng zoomed after him in a separate car but stayed only a few minutes in Tiananmen Square. Inside one bus, Zhao gripped a red loudspeaker and pleaded with the demonstrators to go home. "You're still young; think of the future," he said tearfully, apparently aware that the opportunity for dialogue had passed and that China's leaders had opted for an iron-fisted solution. "We've come too late, we've come too late," he said. But the bleary-eyed students didn't know what Zhao knew or what he meant by those words. Uncomprehending, they clapped respectfully and crowded around Zhao, asking him to sign his autograph on their sleeves and on scraps of cloth. Looking pale and distraught, Zhao left Tiananmen after twenty minutes, returned to Zhongnanhai, and declared he was ill. It was his last public appearance before he officially lost his post on June 23.

Impressed by Zhao's gesture, protest leaders called a meeting at 6:20 A.M. to discuss its significance. Over the broadcasting system, they counseled demonstrators to avoid inflammatory remarks attacking government leaders. Between 9 and 10 P.M., they decided to end the hunger strike. But many students wanted to maintain it, so some went on despite signs of an impending crackdown. That day, Li Peng had dropped the first public hint when he told a visiting Australian delegation, "Chaos has occurred in Beijing, and the Chinese government will take measures to stop it."

MARTIAL LAW

Shortly after midnight on May 20, martial law was declared in Beijing. Li

Peng and Yang Shangkun appeared on television and declared that "government work, school classes, transportation, and factory shifts have become chaotic and anarchic." They announced that soldiers were entering the city to relieve local police exhausted by nonstop riot duty. Li accused protestors of attempting to set up opposition parties and of "beating, smashing, and looting" in other parts of the country. The audience was a sober gathering of top-ranking political and military leaders, with Zhao conspicuously absent. Other Politburo members had asked Zhao to chair the meeting; he had refused even to attend.

About one hundred and fifty thousand troops were mobilized for action. But when they attempted to enter Beijing under the cover of darkness early on May 20, a dazzling display of "people power" blocked the way. Across the city, citizens dragged anything they could find into the streets: huge mobile construction cranes and cement mixers, bits of sewer pipe and city buses arranged in a zig-zag pattern, street dividers and park benches.

The soldiers were confused about their mission. Some had been told they were headed for a training exercise or were making a film. Others had orders to quell a "counter-revolutionary riot" and had been barred from reading newspapers for several days; they were shocked to see how much public support the protest had gathered. An isolated incident of violence erupted in Haidian district – part of Beijing's university belt – when demonstrators attempting to block army convoys clashed with police, injuring forty-five people. For the most part, however, encounters were surprisingly cordial.

At a key crossroads in the Hujialou area, civilians delivered political lectures to soldiers stalled in their six-wheeler trucks. They read newspapers aloud to the troops, treated them to food and water, even asked monitors of the Tiananmen strike committee to help find public toilets for them. One demonstrator stood atop a city bus and urged the crowd through a loudspeaker "not to clash with the PLA."

In the square, the mood was grim. Protestors booed and hissed as Li Peng's speech rasped over the loudspeaker system. Exhausted demonstrators slept on the avenue while vehicles whizzed past their heads. Rumors buzzed. The soldiers will attack at 2 A.M., or at 4:30 A.M., by way of the underground subway, or through the Great Hall of the People. Protestors carried wet gauze masks to protect against tear gas.

The tense night of May 19–20 passed with standoffs at many crucial intersections around Beijing. At daybreak some military trucks packed with soldiers reversed and returned to their bases, including one fifty-truck caravan with about two thousand troops that had been stalled in the west. Crowds cheered wildly and waved V signs, embracing soldiers. At Hujialou, an officer told citizens as his troops departed, "We are soldiers of the people and will never suppress the people." Some of the troops wept with emotion.

The dramatic encounters underscored the PLA's historical relationship with the Chinese masses. The late Chairman Mao Zedong and his revolutionary colleagues shaped the Red Army, later the People's Liberation Army, as an army of the people, largely to discredit abusive and corrupt Chinese Nationalist troops. As a result of that successful hearts-and-minds approach, Chinese civilians had traditionally regarded the PLA with kinship and respect rarely felt for a military body.

But the martial law declaration intensified tensions within the ranks. As far as China's hard-line leaders were concerned, soldiers already in place in Beijing were of suspect loyalty. Earlier that week, nearly one thousand PLA personnel, mostly noncombatants, had marched in protest. The commander of the Beijing-based 38th Army reportedly resigned rather than suppress the uprising. More than one hundred officers of the 38th Army signed a letter vowing to disobey any orders to crack down. One officer from the unit had said, "We want democracy and freedom too."

Deng, as head of the Central Military Commission, wielded vast control over the 3.2-million-strong PLA. He shuttled to various military commands to exercise that clout. Another key figure was Yang Shangkun, Deng's deputy on the military commission. Yang's brother headed the PLA political department. His reputed son-in-law was the chief of staff. And his nephew allegedly commanded the ruthless 27th Army, selected for its loyalty to the Yangs. Demonstrators had accused Yang of running the PLA like a personal fiefdom. "The army belongs to the people, not to Yang Shangkun," said a poster in the middle of Tiananmen Square. China's power struggle raged in the tense days that followed. The hard-line triumvirate of Deng Xiaoping, Yang Shangkun, and Li Peng attempted to drum up support for a purge of Zhao and his liberal followers. In one party meeting, Deng said of Zhao, "He is anti-party, he is counter-revolutionary." China's paramount leader warned that unrest had threatened a decade of reform, but predicted, "Victory is at hand."

Held under virtual house arrest, Zhao nonetheless retained the sympathy of many party members. Although many cadres agreed he had breached party discipline, even top-ranking party leaders in a meeting of about one hundred central committee members were reluctant to label Zhao counter-revolutionary, which brings with it expulsion from the party and criminal proceedings. In work units and academic institutions, political commissars who read aloud secret party documents accusing Zhao of "anti-party" activity were received with some snickers and boos from the back rows.

By the end of May, the Tiananmen fiesta had dwindled to just a few thousand participants. Its tents and buses had become a malodorous shantytown. Protest leader Chai Ling, one of several key student representatives, was depressed about what lay ahead. "I feel very sad," she told an interviewer, "The next step is bloodshed. Only when the square is washed in blood will the people of the whole country wake up."

Still, spirits lifted perceptibly on May 30, when students and faculty from the Central Academy of Arts unveiled a thirty-three-foot-tall "Goddess of Democracy," reminiscent of the Statue of Liberty, made of plaster and styrofoam. Bystanders flocked to the plaza to see the defiant white statue facing down a giant portrait of Mao. Government officials denounced the statue as "a humiliation of the Chinese nation in such a solemn place" and ordered its removal. Many Beijing students wanted to return to campus; but out-of-town protestors unwilling to head home voted to stay on in the square.

There were ominous portents of hard-line resolve. Authorities quietly arrested three Beijing workers from the autonomous workers' association. Police also detained eleven members of the Flying Tigers motorbike brigade, who had acted as look-outs for the students. Perhaps most worrying, party security boss Qiao Shi had stressed to a closed meeting in late May the need for a show of muscle in order to bolster unity and morale within the army. He warned, "It will not do if the PLA does not enter the city."

THE MASSACRE

On the balmy evening of June 2, student leaders in the square picked up a hint that something was brewing. They apprehended a couple of plainclothes police who carried documents indicating that a troop deployment would be launched against the demonstrators. "At first I couldn't believe our government would be so inhuman as to send soldiers to the square to attack our students," said one spokesman for the protestors. Many protestors believed the army's main weapon would be tear gas and prepared yet again to don their surgical masks.

The attack began ignominiously, with a baffling incident after midnight on June 3. Five thousand young, inexperienced soldiers suddenly marched from the east, five abreast, down Changan Avenue toward Tiananmen Square. A human blockade of Beijing citizens stopped them a kilometer short of the square. There was pushing and shoving; the mainly unarmed soldiers were mauled, bruised, scratched. They were frightened. Some milled about in confusion, some wept tears of frustration and bewilderment.

Additional columns converging on the square from the west and south were similarly blocked, though not before a military jeep plowed into protestors' barricades west of the square, leaving three demonstrators dead. These were the first major casualties in seven weeks of nonviolent protest.

The soldiers seemed curiously ill-prepared. Some had marched four hours before reaching the center of the capital. They were laden with camp gear, canteens, ponchos, and knapsacks stuffed with belongings. Once again, civilians plied the dejected troops with political lectures. Some soldiers said they had no clear orders; others were told they were out to counter "bad elements" and "hooligans." The troops were clearly green and disoriented. "Which direction is this anyway?" burst out one soldier with a thick provincial accent. The crowd patiently explained where he was.

Chai Ling, Wu'er Kaixi, and Wang Dan, the three acknowledged leaders of the student movement, conduct a meeting in Tiananmen Square. Following the military crackdown, Chai Ling went into hiding; Wu'er Kaixi fled the country; and Wang Dan, a history student, was arrested. <PT>

The dispirited soldiers had retreated by midmorning. But the mood had clearly turned sour. China's hardliners cited the PLA's humiliation – and the loss of some AK-47 assault rifles and ammunition after soldiers abandoned vehicles – as reason to get tough. "Recover the square at any cost," Deng reportedly said.

In the afternoon, violent incidents erupted west of Tiananmen Square.

Near the Great Hall of the People, about five thousand soldiers beat demonstrators who tried to block them. Shortly afterward, soldiers fired tear gas cannisters at crowds marching on the Communist party headquarters. Protestors responded by hurling bricks and rocks at soldiers and military vehicles. Soldiers lashed back with truncheons and belts.

Early that evening, state television and radio stations broadcast grim warnings. "Do not come into the streets, do not go to Tiananmen Square," residents were told, "stay at home to safeguard your lives." The killing began in earnest around 10 P.M., when gunfire rang out along Changan Avenue four or five kilometers west of the square. Troops armed with AK-47 assault rifles moved toward the heart of the protest in armored vehicles and trucks, firing as they advanced.

That triggered a paroxysm of carnage and cruelty, which raged until dawn. Howling residents stood up to the soldiers with rocks, pipes, and primitive gasoline bombs. Just after midnight, two armored personnel carriers rumbling down Changan Avenue toward the square from the east were ambushed by protestors tossing Molotov cocktails. The crew of one flaming vehicle jumped out, said a witness, and one of the soldiers was torn limb from limb by the frenzied crowd.

Some of the worst bloodshed took place between midnight and 2 A.M. west of the square on Changan Avenue. Soldiers fought pitched battles with defiant crowds near the Muxidi bridge. Tanks smashed into barriers. Buses and military vehicles burned at intersections, highlighting the orgy of violence with orange flames and flickering shadows. This time the soldiers were not green youth, but hardened veterans. The 27th Army, blindly loyal to Yang Shangkun, committed the worst of the atrocities. At one point, the units' armored vehicles ran over fellow soldiers from a supporting unit who had not been nimble enough to step out of the way. Nearby hospitals quickly filled up with the dead and wounded, their hallways awash with blood. By

3 A.M., a line of troops had blocked Changan Avenue at the northeast corner of the square, just down from the Beijing Hotel. Demonstrators taunted them from about fifty meters away. The soldiers assumed firing positions – then shot directly into the crowd. Dozens of bodies fell, and the casualties were spirited away on tricycle carts. Again the line of death formed, and again gunfire crackled above the pandemonium. The grisly ritual repeated itself for hours.

Almost to the end, the students believed they could prevail. Taiwan-born pop singer Hou Dejian and others negotiated with soldiers for an orderly departure from Tiananmen Square. At about 4 A.M., as the staccato of gunfire drew nearer from the northwest, electric lights in the square suddenly went out. About two hundred troops, bayonets at the ready, filed out of the Great Hall of the People and took up positions south of the obelisk. Huddled around it, protestors began to withdraw as a gray dawn broke over Beijing. "We can't let any more blood flow," a voice came over the student broadcasting system, "we must leave." About one thousand protestors filed out to the south, many weeping, some singing the *Internationale*. At first, the protestors were directed by relatively professional paratroop units. But when some weary protestors walked past the Beijing concert hall, a different group of soldiers in armored vehicles opened fire, and many demonstrators fell.

Meanwhile, a convoy of about fifty trucks, tanks, and armored personnel carriers clanked in from the northeast shortly after 5 A.M. The tracked vehicles chewed up Changan Avenue, smashing through barricades and spitting random gunfire. Someone shouted, "Beasts! You're inhuman!" Others silently wept. Tricycle carts sped past with bleeding victims. Turning into the square at high speed, the armored vehicles rumbled over anything that stood in the way: tents, bodies, the Goddess of Democracy, apparently even protestors who had tried to hold out inside their crude shelters.

By 7 A.M., loudspeakers in the square declared, "The rebellion has been suppressed." But bullets continued to crackle throughout the morning of June 4, as the lines of soldiers northeast of the square fired repeatedly at citizens congregating in the street near the Beijing Hotel. After one midmorning volley, about thirty bodies littered the boulevard. When Chinese tried to remove the casualties, they were gunned down, too.

The carnage was so shocking that many Beijing residents refused to believe the PLA would tolerate it. Rumors of civil war circulated as tanks assumed defensive positions on a crucial intersection near the diplomatic compound of Jianguomenwai. But the confrontation never materialized. Instead, soldiers stationed at the intersection opened fire on the diplomatic compound. Officers said they were targeting snipers who had shot three soldiers. But foreign diplomats speculated the blatant attack was a retaliation for the flight of dissident astrophysicist Fang Lizhi into the American Embassy to seek refuge.

The shooting incident at Jianguomenwai triggered a mass evacuation of foreign residents. With gasoline scarce and troop patrols moving throughout the city, departing passengers ran a tense gauntlet to the airport. Chinese soldiers stopped a van of Americans and took their money, luggage, and tickets. The foreigners had to walk for an hour to reach the terminal. Others were equally terrified by the sights in town. "There was a soldier's body, burned, hanging from a bridge," said an Australian tourist. "That made me get out of there."

Even as the violence began to subside, Beijing remained a nightmare world of grief and destruction. At hospitals and makeshift morgues, relatives sobbed over the dead and dying. Burned city buses and other wreckage littered major crossroads. West of Tiananmen Square stretched a wasteland of gutted military vehicles, including dozens of mangled trucks and more than sixty torched armored personnel carriers. At Beijing Normal University, a white vertical banner of the sort displayed at funerals declared: "A generation of younger heroes has gone to an early death."

BIG BROTHER IS WATCHING

The government unleashed a reign of terror to uproot remnants of the democracy movement. Police searched house to house and made mass arrests. Within a month after the massacre, thirty people had been sentenced to death – and executed, with a single shot to the head – on charges of arson, destruction of state property, and other "counter-revolutionary" actions. Eighteen special hotlines for informants were set up, and Chinese were exhorted to snitch. One student leader was turned in by his own sister. But some informants were not exactly cooperative; they phoned in the names of Deng Xiaoping and Li Peng as notorious murderers.

One man was convicted after a video clip of him being interviewed by American television flashed across the Chinese evening news. The footage, which was pirated as ABC transmitted it out of Beijing, showed him stating, "They killed twenty thousand people ... you've never seen anything like it." A superimposed caption in Chinese asked residents to turn him in to the nearest Public Security Bureau. Within hours of seeing the news item, two women in the port city Dalian did just that. He was sentenced to ten years in prison for rumor-mongering.

The government's "big lie" campaign insisted only about three hundred people – including just thirty-six students – had died, mostly troops killed by counter-revolutionary "thugs." (The real figure may never be known; the best estimates ran between seven hundred and twenty-six hundred.) To bolster the government's version of the incident, Chinese television aired selectively edited footage that showed wild-eyed protestors brandishing weapons, torching vehicles, and beating hapless soldiers. The fear campaign had a chilling effect, dampening contacts between Chinese and foreigners. "Go home quickly, you're not safe here," hissed a Chinese man who had sidled up to a foreigner as both pedaled bicycles along Changan Avenue a

few d
done.
back.
cadre
to ma
no re
virtua
of to
...to

De
massa
an o
China
recoi
hype
panie
territ
of th
and

W
stude
large
man
One
sout
back
in J
to W

S
psyc
dipl
relea
as s
beg
the
Lin

W
to 2
pub
dict
said
ove

re

In their dormitory rooms, student organizers write posters to announce the time and place of demonstrations and to disseminate their views. <DT>

PAGE 48:

A young Chinese couple wheels down Changan Avenue, Beijing's main thoroughfare. Their lifestyle is one response to a decade of economic reform and China's opening to the West. <PT>

PAGE 49:

At dawn, elderly Chinese still gather in parks to practice the ancient exercise of Tai Ji Quan. <PT>

PAGES 50 AND 51:

At Beijing University, crowds of students press forward to read and record messages. Posters became both a symbol and a catalyst of the student movement. <PT>

In a square behind the Forbidden City, two veteran players go head to head during their daily game of Chinese checkers. <PT>

Couples dance the jitterbug in Ritan Park before going to work in the morning. Both the fashion and the beat reflect China's growing cultural freedom and social diversity. <PT>

Students surround Hu Yaobang's portrait with funeral wreaths at the Monument to People's Heroes in Tiananmen Square. Two years before his death on April 15, Hu's liberalism had won him student support and caused his removal as Communist party secretary. <PT>

As the official funeral ceremony is conducted in the Great Hall of the People, police and students face each other in the square nearby. <PT>

Massive marches frequently swept through Beijing in late April and May. Behind their banner, minority students from the Central Institute of Nationalities join the thousands gathering in Tiananmen Square. <PT>

Police attempting to seal off Tiananmen Square are overwhelmed by demonstrators, whose number grew in response to an April 26 People's Daily *editorial that called the movement "a handful of people conspiring to create turmoil."* <PT>

In the morning sunlight of April 22, students who disobeyed a government ban and spent the night before Hu Yaobang's funeral in Tiananmen Square savor a moment of triumph. <PT>

FACING PAGE:

Heads bowed before their handwritten eulogies, mourners maintain a peaceful vigil in the hours before the funeral ceremony. <PT>

In a cramped dormitory room at Beijing University, students relax during a break from the demonstrations. University dormitory rooms of this size usually house up to six students. <PT>

FACING PAGE:

A demonstrator exhorts fellow students occupying Tiananmen Square. Among the reforms called for were press freedom and an end to official corruption and nepotism. <PT>

PAGE 64 AND 65:

A dormitory washroom at Beijing University. Even at China's most prestigious schools, conditions are spartan; still, competition for admission is intense. <PT>

Deng Xiaoping, China's paramount leader, links arms with Soviet leader Mikhail Gorbachev and his wife, Raisa, in Beijing on May 16. This historic summit meeting ending years of Sino-Soviet estrangement was upstaged by student demonstrators, whose presence in Tiananmen Square forced the official state welcome to be held at the airport. <PT>

FACING PAGE:

Science and technology students are among the multitude parading past Mao Zedong's portrait at the Gate of Heavenly Peace during the summit. It was here, at the northern end of Tiananmen Square, that Mao declared the founding of the People's Republic of China in 1949 and where, during the height of the Cultural Revolution in 1966, he waved his support to millions of Red Guards. <PT>

Student leaders call for a hunger strike to dramatize their cause and gain wider support. This marked a turning point in the movement's size and strength. <PT>

Members of a newly formed workers' organization arrive in a factory truck to support the students. The hunger strike, begun on May 13 just before the Gorbachev visit, galvanized Beijing residents. The workers' group has since been outlawed. <PT>

FACING PAGE:

Intellectuals – teachers, journalists, writers, and filmmakers – show their sympathy for the students. By mid-May, the hunger strikers had become a magnet, attracting the support of many groups. <PT>

PAGES 72 AND 73:

Bus riders stare out at the growing spectacle in Beijing's streets. Nothing like it had been seen in the forty years of Communist rule. <PT>

Students shout pro-democracy slogans in Tiananmen Square. They now demanded a substantive dialogue with the government and official recognition as a legal, patriotic movement. <DT>

FACING PAGE:

Student banners display tears and blood as symbols of dedication to the movement. During the hunger strike, students and their supporters had begun to occupy the square around the clock. <PT>

PAGES 76 AND 77:

A hunger striker is rushed from the square by fellow students and volunteer medical workers. Some three thousand students from universities in Beijing participated in the hunger strike, which lasted seven days. <PT>

PAGES 78 AND 79:

Like many mothers, this woman views the events in Tiananmen Square with concern for the safety of the young people. <DT>

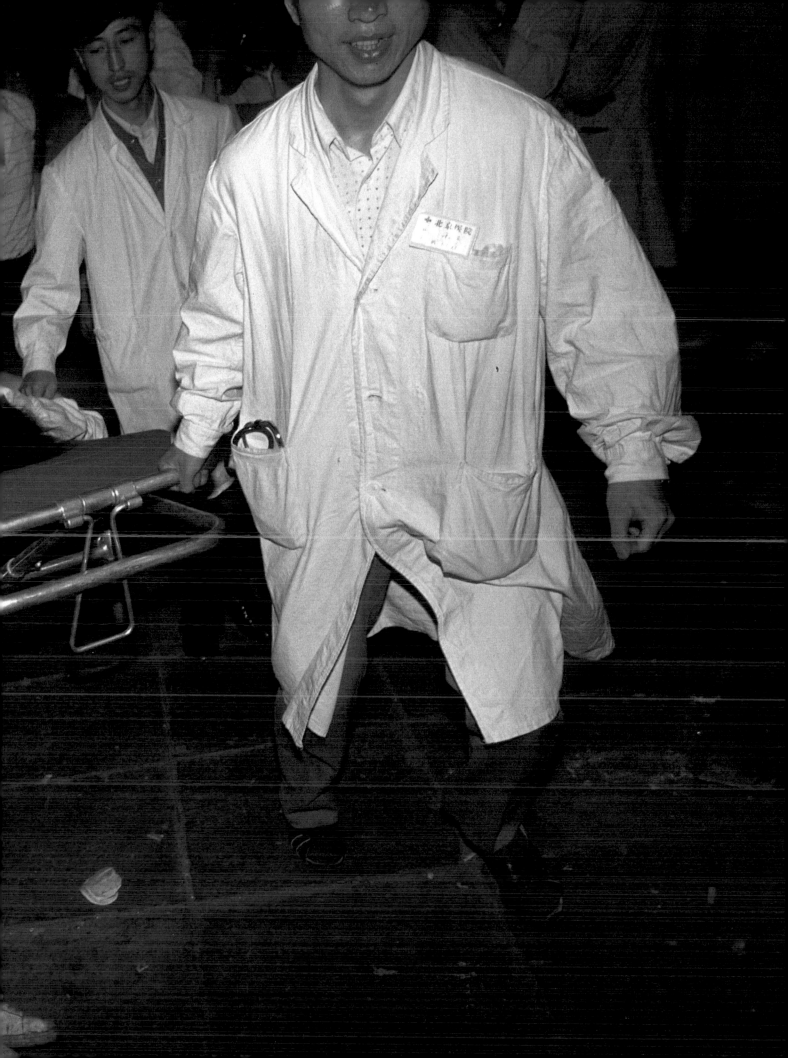

Student hunger strikers seek comfort in books and each other's arms. <PT>

FACING PAGE:

One of twelve students from the Central Drama Academy who refused even water during the hunger strike collapses in the arms of medics. <PT>

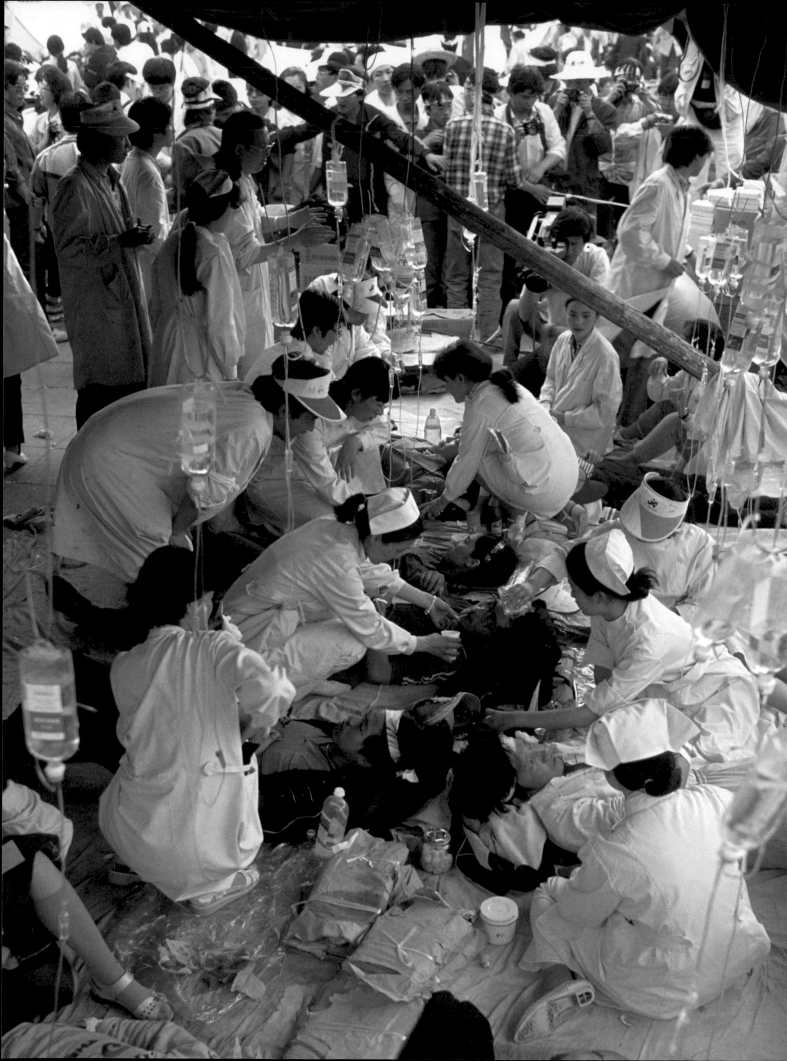

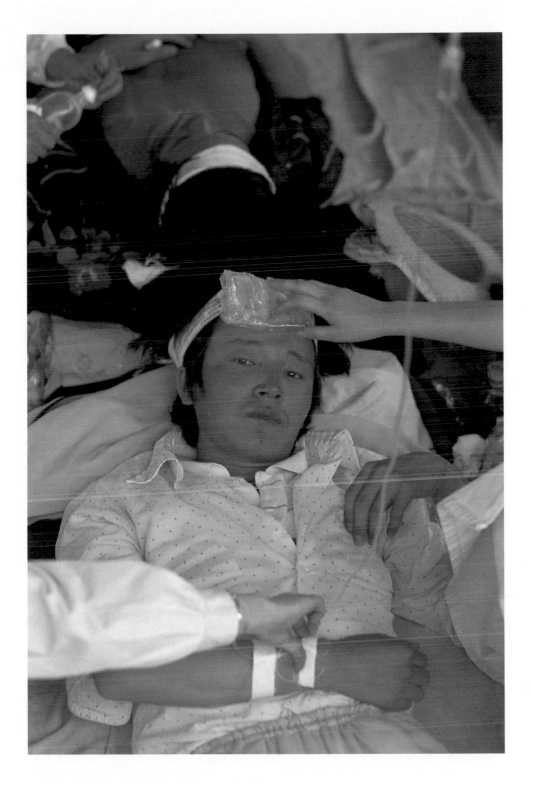

A hunger striker, weak but defiant, receives medical treatment. On May 18, a nationally televised meeting between representatives of the hunger strikers and Prime Minister Li Peng ended in discord. <PT>

FACING PAGE:

A makeshift field hospital is set up in Tiananmen Square. <PT>

A truckload of Beijing policemen enters the square to salute the students and show their support. On the night of May 19, students ended the hunger strike but not the occupation of the square. <PT>

FACING PAGE:

Workers appear at factory windows to watch and sometimes to encourage the masses headed for Tiananmen Square. The next day, May 20, the government declared martial law. <PT>

PAGES 86 AND 87:

Hours after martial law is declared, a human wall of resistance meets a troop convoy attempting to enter central Beijing. <PT>

At the western edge of Beijing, a young woman climbs onto the hood of an army truck with an emotional plea to soldiers not to move against the students. <PT>

PAGE 90:

A Beijing policeman joins the student demonstration in defiance of martial law orders. The sign in his hand reads: "Students will surely win." <PT>

PAGE 91:

On the second day of martial law, a student blocks the path of an army truck on the outskirts of Beijing. Such standoffs happened repeatedly and prevented troops from entering the city for two weeks. <PT>

Students besiege soldiers of the People's Liberation Army (PLA) with words, explaining their cause. Many soldiers were said to be ignorant of why they were sent to Beijing, believing they were part of a military exercise. <PT>

In an expression of appeasement and goodwill, students offer steamed buns to stalled soldiers. Traditionally, the PLA has enjoyed the respect and support of the people. <PT>

FACING PAGE:

Weary PLA soldiers with automatic weapons await orders after their convoy is stopped by students on the edge of Beijing. <PT>

FACING PAGE:

As they turn away from Beijing, soldiers reach out through the canvas cover of their truck to shake hands with students. <PT>

PAGE 98:

Students of Beijing University, Beijing Agriculture University, and Qinghua University, China's MIT, fly their school banners as the sun sets behind the Great Hall of the People. Students now lived in the square, while troops were encamped on the outskirts of Beijing. <PT>

PAGE 99:

In response to martial law, caricatures of Prime Minister Li Peng and President Yang Shangkun call for their removal from office. Within the Communist party leadership, there was a fierce struggle between the hardliners and the supporters of Zhao Ziyang, the more liberal party secretary. <PT>

PAGES 100 AND 101:

A couple in Tiananmen Square spends a thoughtful moment amid the spirited resistance to martial law and the uncertainty of where it might lead. <DT>

In their shared purpose and joyous mood, students in the square formed a sense of community. <PT>

FACING PAGE:

Students from other cities and provinces swell the ranks of demonstrators in Beijing. Among the sea of banners, one message expressed the theme of the movement: "Power Belongs to the People!" <PT>

Students take shelter in a tent, discussing the day's events over a thermos and the Beijing Evening News. By late May, students were debating if and when they should end their sit-in. <PT>

FACING PAGE:

A broken umbrella is a student's only protection during an early summer storm sweeping through the square. <PT>

PAGES 106 AND 107:

The face of a young woman reflects apprehension as marchers continue through the streets of Beijing. <DT>

Students from outside Beijing camp under a sculpture of revolutionary heroes in front of Mao Zedong's Mausoleum at the south end of Tiananmen Square. <DT>

FACING PAGE:

Chai Ling, a prominent student leader, holds an intense conversation in the square. A twenty-three-year-old graduate student in psychology at Beijing Normal University, Chai Ling was elected Commander of the Headquarters to Defend Tiananmen Square. <PT>

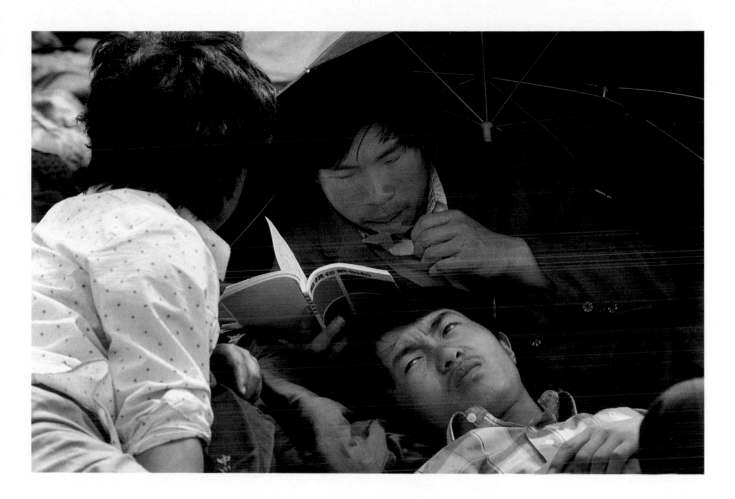

Under a hot sun, students read and wait. The occupation of Tiananmen Square became a war of nerves between demonstrators and the government, each waiting to see what the other would do. On May 29, students voted not to leave the square until a session of the National People's Congress, scheduled for June 20. <DT>

FACING PAGE:

Students settle in areas according to their respective schools. In some ways, the square took on the life of a small city. <DT>

Chai Ling's husband, Feng Congde (on the right), also a member of the student leadership, finds respite in a tent that became the central headquarters on the square. Donations of tents, clothing, and food from local residents and organizations, and from Chinese overseas, helped sustain the students. <DT>

PAGE 114:

A young woman provides a drink of water for her boyfriend after a night's sleep atop a public bus. The buses were pulled into the square during the hunger strike to provide shelter for the demonstrators, and remained there until a few days after martial law was declared. <DT>

PAGE 115:

A student walks past a line of buses. The accumulation of garbage posed another health problem. <PT>

Sanitation workers sweep around students asleep in cotton quilts on the pavement of Tiananmen Square. <PT>

PAGES 118 AND 119:
Students at the Central Academy of Arts build the Goddess of Democracy. The statue was carried on tricycle carts in three parts to Tiananmen Square and erected on May 30. <DT>

A student lookout helps guard the Goddess of Democracy in the square. When the government warned that the statue would be removed, students circled it with tents and vowed to protect it. <DT>

FACING PAGE:

Students hurry to protect the Goddess of Democracy from a threatening windstorm. The statue's face and hairstyle bear the distinctive look of martyrs in Chinese art. The gown and arms holding the torch resemble the Statue of Liberty in New York Harbor. <DT>

PAGES 124 AND 125:

With government pressure increasing, speakers address the crowd in Tiananmen Square on strategies for preserving the democracy movement. Students used microphones and cassette players to record the events for their own newspaper and loudspeaker systems in the square. <DT>

Students and Beijing residents shout their indignation at unarmed soldiers who tried to enter Tiananmen Square in the early hours of June 3. The troops — thousand of them — wore white shirts and green uniform pants; they were stopped just one kilometer from the square. <DT>

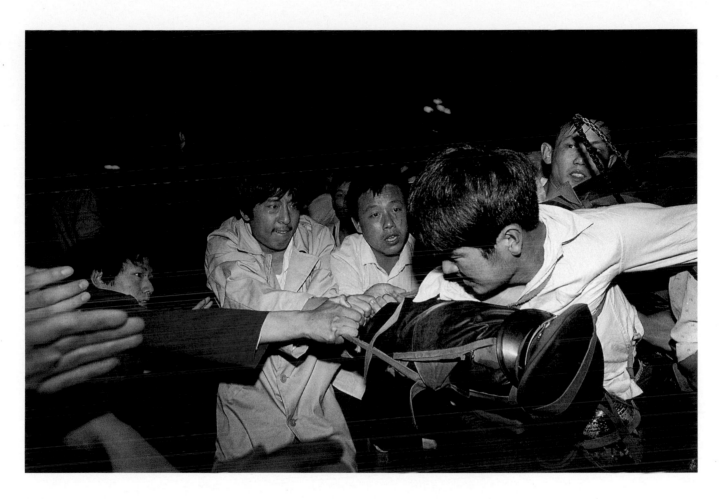

A soldier is pulled from his unit and held by student resisters. <DT>

Students besieged the soldiers for hours, and the troops were forced to retreat. They abandoned their vehicles, some of which contained weapons and other supplies. <DT>

PAGES 130 AND 131:

In the early morning darkness of June 3, the young soldiers appear bewildered and defeated. <DT>

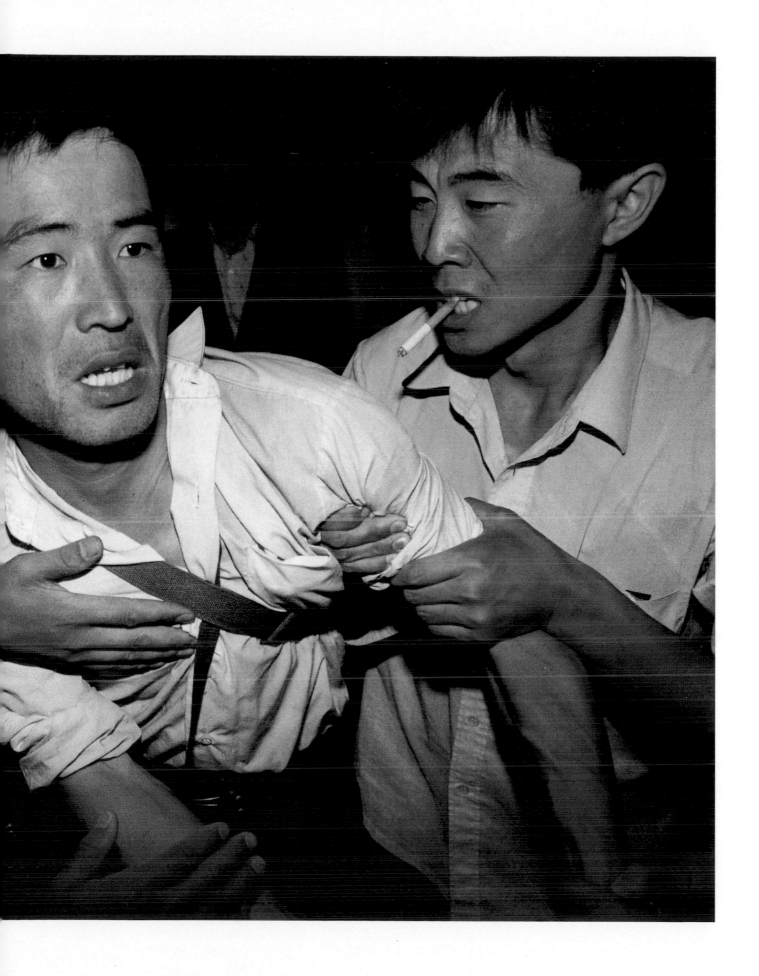

Military helmets, shoes, and license plates from the troops who retreated are displayed as trophies. <DT>

FACING PAGE:
New troops emerged in front of the Great Hall of the People later on June 3 at the west end of Tiananmen Square. Just hours before the crackdown, a woman appeals to soldiers in a troop carrier stopped by the crowds. <DT>

A man leads the demonstrators in chants against the new troops. The situation became increasingly tense, heightened by rumors that the military might take the square by force. <DT>

PAGES 136 AND 137:

A young man holds his blood-soaked shirt after an encounter with troops. In contrast with the soldiers forced to retreat the night before, these were veteran troops in battle gear. <DT>

On the night of June 3, a young man lies dead on Changan Avenue, crushed by an armored personnel carrier. The APCs had roared past military convoys stalled by the demonstrators, leaving behind this victim and an angry crowd of thousands. <DT>

PAGES 140 THROUGH 143:

Wounded civilians are carried away as soldiers fire into the crowd during an assault that lasted several hours. By the early morning of June 4, the army had made its way into Tiananmen Square. As thousands of soldiers lined up across Changan Avenue at the northern end of the square, thousands of civilians would surge forward in an apparent attempt to re-enter the square, taunting soldiers, as if refusing to believe the army would fire against them. Volleys of gunfire rang out every ten minutes, sending the crowd running for cover. People would then rush back, some collecting bodies of the dead and wounded, then retreat again when the gunfire resumed. Changan Avenue, in every direction, became a battleground. <DT>

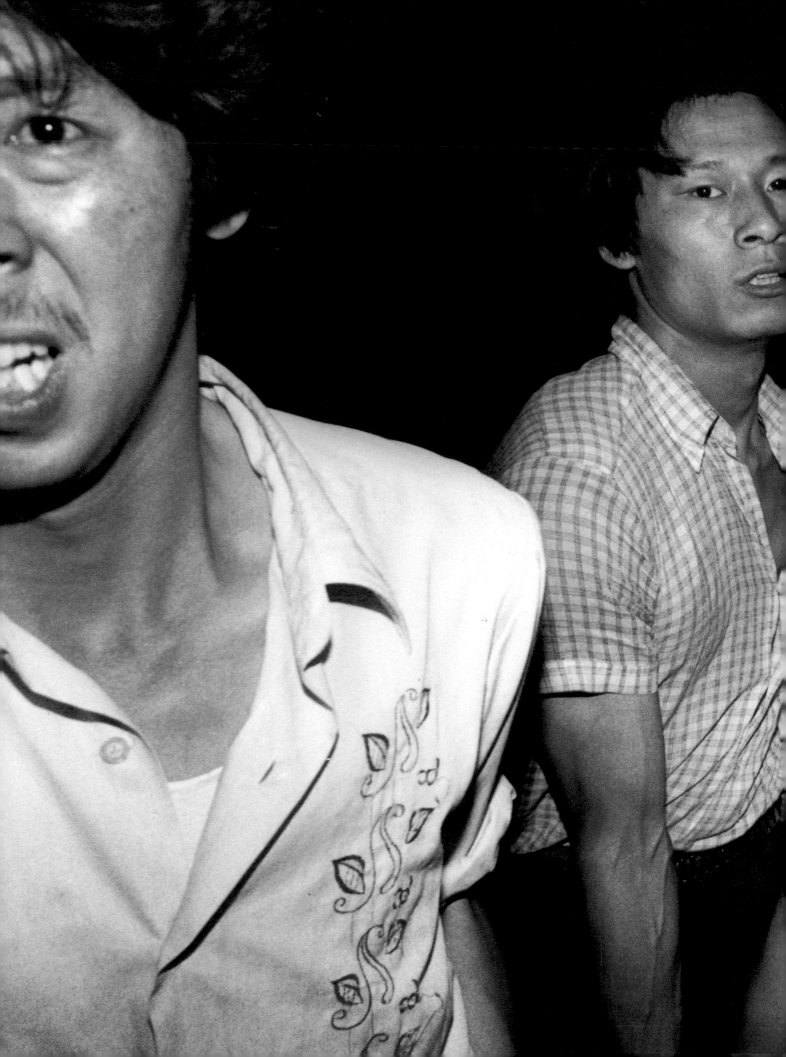

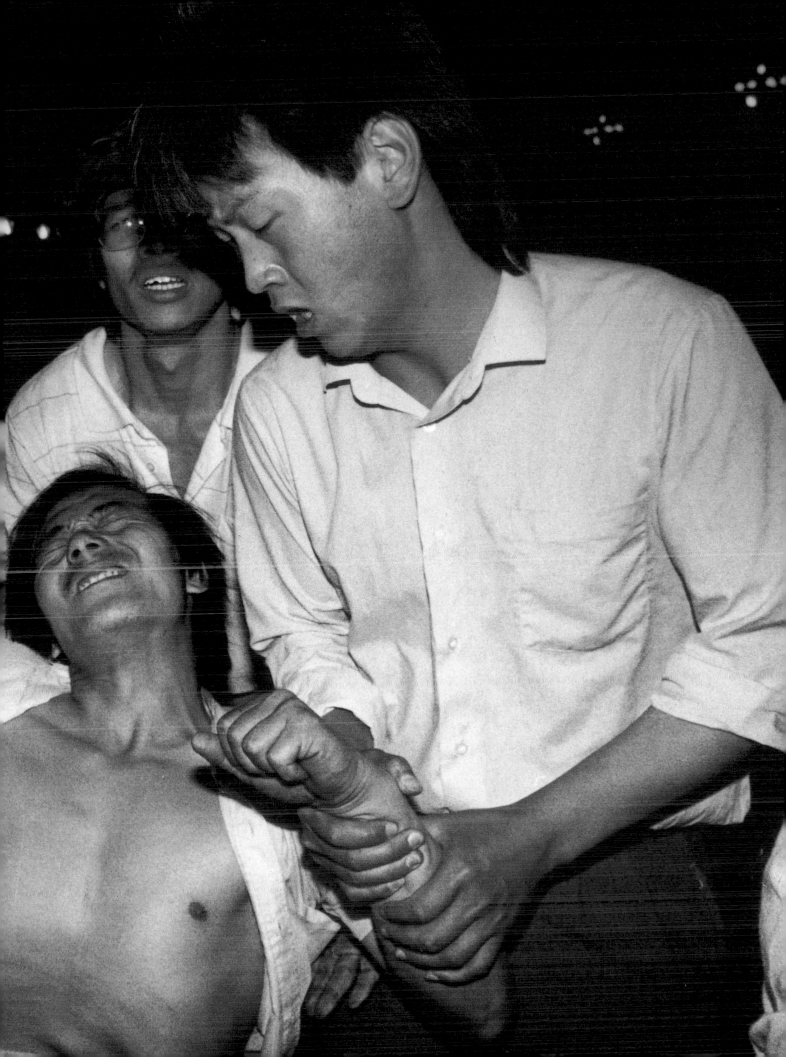

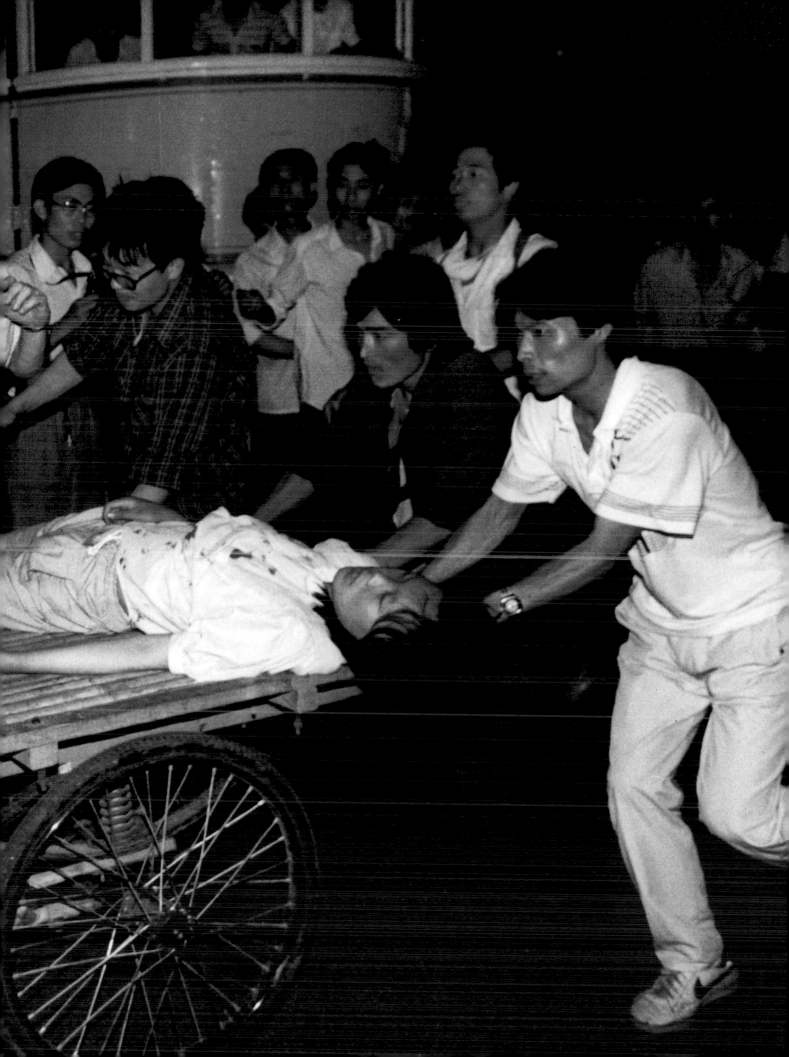

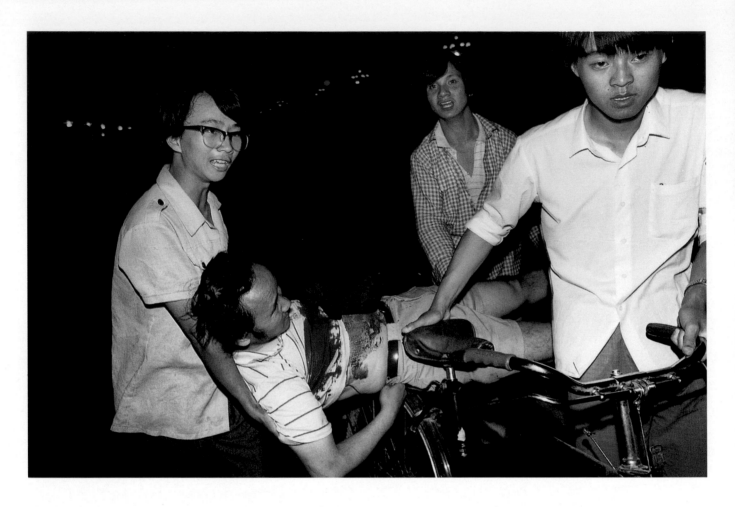

Friends remove the wounded from the front line. <DT>

Carts and bicycles become makeshift ambulances. <DT>

PAGES 146 AND 147:

As people around him fall dead and wounded in the army attack, a young man sits down in the middle of the street to cry. <DT>

PAGES 148 AND 149:

Soldiers and tanks maintain their position on Changan Avenue, on the northern perimeter of Tiananmen Square, where in the pre-dawn hours troops opened fire on thousands of defiant civilians. <DT>

PAGES 150 AND 151:

A truck burns in the evening twilight of June 4, set afire by angry students. Outraged by the massacre, students and their supporters made trucks and buses frequent targets of retaliation. <PT>

PAGES 152 AND 153:

At a hospital just blocks from Tiananmen Square in the hours following the start of the army crackdown, a room becomes a morgue. <PT>

A mother learns of the death of her son, a university student in Beijing. <DT>

A woman grieves for her younger brother, a victim of the massacre. The government admitted that more than two hundred civilians had died, including thirty-six students. Other estimates ranged from several hundred into the thousands. <DT>

PAGES 158 AND 159:
Pedestrians and bicyclists maneuver past a convoy of burned-out trucks and armored personnel carriers on western Changan Avenue. The military vehicles apparently were abandoned by soldiers and later set afire by citizens. <PT>

On Changan Avenue, the remains of bicycles adorn a burned tank on which angry citizens have painted a swastika. The bicycles were used as makeshift barriers against military convoys. <PT>

A man sits amid the debris of a deserted western Changan Avenue, two days after the army assault. Impressions of tank treads can be seen across broken traffic signs, one of which still reads "order." <DT>

PAGES 162 AND 163:

The charred remains of a bus, next to billboards advertising consumer goods and a new film, stand a few blocks from Tiananmen Square. <PT>

Soldiers move into battle position outside the diplomatic compound on eastern Changan Avenue. Soldiers fired directly into buildings, claiming they were returning sniper fire. The incident provoked a strong diplomatic protest. <PT>

With a bush as cover, this picture was taken of an armored personnel carrier roaming Changan Avenue and firing at random. <DT>

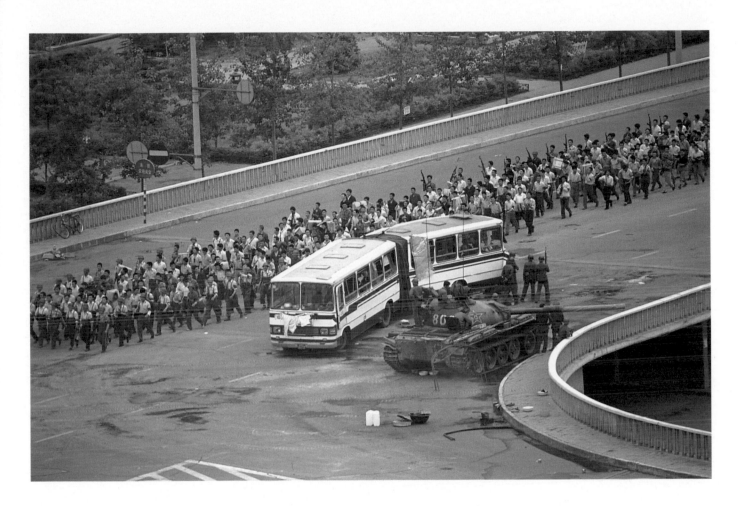

A militia unit passes soldiers on Changan Avenue. The authorities tried to mobilize popular support against the student leaders, intellectuals, and workers active in the protest movement, who also became the object of a nationwide roundup. <PT>

FACING PAGE:

Soldiers and tanks take a defensive position at the Jianguomenwai overpass of eastern Changan Avenue. There were rumors of a possible clash between army units at odds over the military crackdown. <PT>

PAGES 168 AND 169:

Foreigners crowd into Beijing airport, waiting for flights out of the country. The exodus included business people, tourists, teachers, and students. <DT>

Quiet now, Tiananmen Square is guarded by tanks and soldiers of the People's Liberation Army stationed in front of the Gate of Heavenly Peace. <DT>

The Goddess of Democracy came to represent the hopes and aspirations of the student movement. The statue had stood only four days in Tiananman Square before it was destroyed by soldiers on June 4. <DT>